Transcendent Keys to Power

By

Daniel Updike

This book is dedicated to:

My beloved wife who has stood by me through thick and thin not only in the writing of this book, but in life as my partner. Words cannot express how much she means to me, and I only hope that my actions tell the tale.

Table of Contents

Introduction

There have been many books written on occult subjects over these years, be they "practical guides"; "grimoires" or general interest works. I have not found very much written for the public that goes into what actually "makes" a sorcerer, magician or witch. I know in my own experience, as a fledgling sorcerer looking in vain for sources that would teach about the prerequisites of magick, though there were quite a few as time went on discussed operational magic. Then and now, I find it quite ironic that such teaching was/is so scarce since operational magic in occultism is continually gaining popularity.

This, in a nutshell, is what has given rise to the book you have in your possession at this moment. I decided that it was about time that a book that talks about prerequisite training which is necessary for consistent success in operational magic be written. I am certainly not "the fount of all wisdom", but for the good of those seriously pursuing the path of the sorcerer, I am willing to share with 30 years of experience in both success and failure bring.

This is NOT a work of "academia" where I go into the endless renditions of other magicians in occult practice. It is the author's conviction that if you are truly motivated for effectiveness in magick, that the reader will already be seeking or already possess at least some of the written works of occult practitioners within that realm of endeavor. THIS book is written in a more "conversational" way, where I believe the most effective presentation of the "transcendent" keys of power can be expressed with the least amount of confusion. Dealing with such esoteric principles confusion is the biggest danger to the reader, as many of the principles talked about (if not ALL) must be EXPERIENCED to be grasped words inevitably fail.

I am going to start out with the most persistent challenge to magical success, which is the indoctrinated inner beliefs we all have been programmed with that are not only a hindrance to successful magic but stops the spiritual evolution of the magician or sorcerer dead cold!

Next, I will address the biggest points of development the magician/sorcerer needs to work on in order to take operational magic and succeed with it in more than a "hit and miss" manner.

I will be including exercises that can be a help in developing these potentials, as well as some online sources that you can view which will augment your practices.

In the last part of the book, the purpose behind magic itself will be discussed. The false dichotomy of what in our day, is called "the right-hand path" and "the left-hand path" will be addressed. The meaning of both "enlightenment" and was commonly referred to as either ascension or "apotheosis" will also be examined.

This book is meant to be a challenge to commonly accepted views, and you may well find yourself re-examining your own worldview as you dive deeper into this text. Do your best to have an open mind and examine yourself for truth as you go through this book.

May you find the undiscovered country in the wild darkness of the infinite!

PART I: De-Programming Yourself

Chapter 1 "Accepting What Is"

The first thing we need to seriously consider is the truth of where one is in the quest for numinous knowledge. We are quite adept at self – deception, even in our day to day lives, and this "quality" is a tremendous hindrance in any magical/occult path as it prevents us from experiencing real growth.

The problem of self-deception is entirely the result of our own original thought processes. A great source of the very foundation of self-deception is the influence and programming that has come from indoctrination which we have all received through the environment we have been born into. This takes on different faces as all of us as individuals have had different challenges, experiences and natural predilections. What these varied stimuli have in common though is a direct falsification of the sense of "self" and what we are in truth.

There are forces that benefit from our remaining in this indoctrinated and programmed state. The consumerist stick societies, governments and religious institutions certainly do!

There are also aspects of our egoic mind that also get a big payoff from this, because if we remain in this preprogram state we can slip into the "us/them" mindset as well as the disempowering "victim/hero" mentality. What is the payoff of this? At the core, the denial of personal responsibility! We can get so carried away with the "causes" we can be a part of; the material possessions we can attain; the "wrongs" we can "right"; that we truly forget where real change comes from. Real change comes from connection to who we ARE, not the false image pre-programmed into us that we "should" be.

Please look at this diagram (figure 1A + figure 1B)

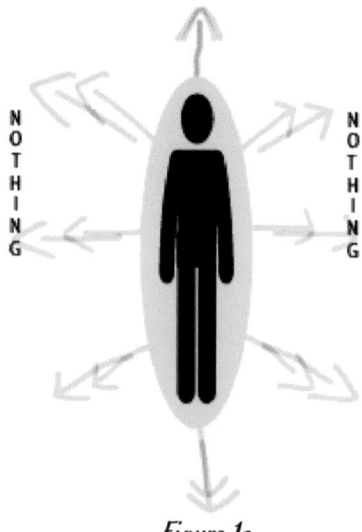

Figure 1a

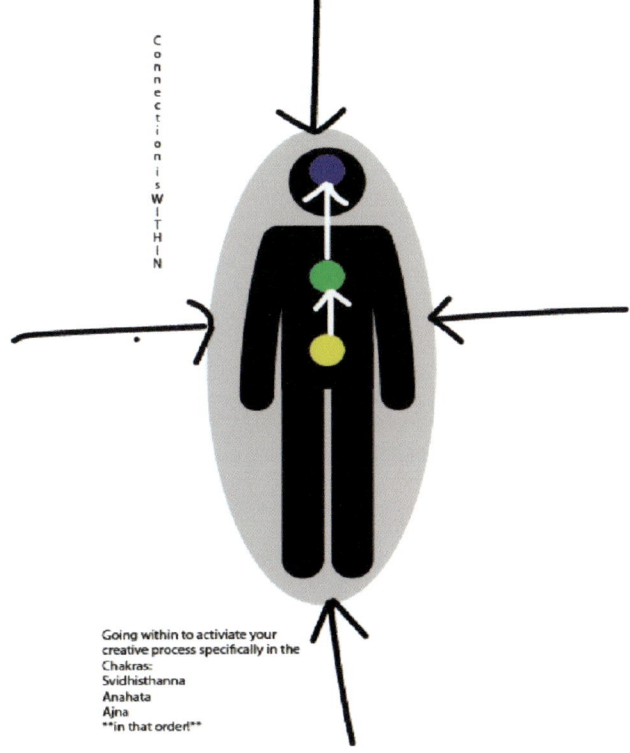

Figure 1b

From these 2 diagrams I want you to see how "what is" gets completely missed when the focused gaze is always outward to what ends up being an empty illusion.

When we with brutal self-honesty turn our gaze inward, we in a PROCESS begin to embody "what is" warts and all. This enables and empowers us to begin the process of ACTUAL transformation which makes a difference not from the outside in, but the INSIDE out!

The process I have described is the starting point for the magician/sorcerer as this path is one of personal transformation. Magic is not the path for you if you have an aversion to change. This path WILL change you whether you like it or not. How it changes you is up to you, either in the transformation to your authentic self, or the disassembly of your personality and utter destruction of your life. I can tell you that with the years of experience that I've had in this art that there is no way that I have found that you can embrace a path of magic without having it affect you on the deepest levels of your being.

The following artistic conception is an example of how energy flows from DARKNESS (the unknown) into manifestation within our awareness. This, of course within the BALANCED energy field of a human soul working in conjunction with the True Self.

**Painted by "Kelly-Kelly"
Used by permission**

Now, without BRUTAL self-honesty this process can be circumvented as mentioned above and brought into the same wild goose chase as the outward focus on what is illusion was talked about above. You may ask, "how do I deal with painful truths I may find out about myself?". You must realize that in being truly honest with ourselves we are going to come across things within that are not only positive and wonderful, but very destructive to the self, possibly embarrassing, and downright painful because we don't want to hear even from within that which disturbs the illusion we have projected about who we think we are. This is normal and a part of the process because if we hold on to false projections we are distracted by illusion and not really affecting any change or influencing the effectiveness of our practice. It is only through acknowledging and accepting these things about ourselves even if we do not like what we see or hear that brings us to the place where we can deal with the root causes and issues that hold us back.

One of the things that is an issue directly related to what I was just talking about is fear, (even if on acknowledge) that I think all of us have which is part of a protection mechanism to preserve our self-image. The mind works in both conscious and subconscious levels to protect us from pain. We must redefine our concept of pain on very deep levels if success is to be achieved.

Modalities of Pain:

Common Understanding

The common understanding of pain is that it is an experience (both physical and psychological) that is unpleasant. Pain can be a warning that something is wrong, or part of us has been or is being harmed either physically or psychologically.

Pain in this context is very valid and needs to be examined as to its source. If the reasons for the pain are true, remedy must be sought to deal with the source is the message of pain is there to help us.

Extended Understanding:

Beyond what has just been discussed, there is ANOTHER source of pain that is mainly psychological but is very different than that which is alerting us to harm. This type of pain has no basis in the legitimate reasons discussed for pain and is the result of THOUGHT.

We are programmed in subtle ways not just from our upbringing, but from evolution on this planet to keep ourselves to what is "familiar"! These things that we experience which are "unfamiliar" create a negative reaction within us in our thought processes and can be interpreted as PAIN psychologically.

Now what happens if what we are familiar with (within this context) is harmful or self-defeating? Our natural tendency is to defend what is "familiar" regardless and become slaves to this type of fear sometimes without even realizing it! Do you see how insidious and detrimental to our evolution and becoming what we are in truth the consumerist, religious and secular programming we have as human beings' generation after generation is? We have been programmed through this vulnerability generation after generation to believe in the easy way, the way of comfort and pleasure (and sometimes this is where we need to be!) And reject those things which do not fall into those categories even if they are things that bring us truth and growth. This programming reinforces the illusion as being reality on the deepest levels when it's really in actuality "relative truth" meaning that it's true for our existence on this planet within this incarnated form, but not truth with a capital "T" which is directly related to the infinite. People will and do rise to fight for their chains as a result of this programming because venturing into the unfamiliar territory of what is outside the confines of our limited understanding holds deep fear and pain to them because it does not fall into the programmed parameters.

Starting this process of inward focus requires, in addition to the self-honesty I've been talking about, a release as well of "self-judgment" which is also part of the mental programming mentioned above intended to bring us by our own accord back into the confines of limitation. This may be challenging at first, as we are conditioned as mentioned above to be "self-critical" in order to strive for what we are taught that we "should" be. Realize that because of this program propensity that the "self-judgment" we would engage in is skewed and distorted. Just release it by a deliberate decision and in your inward focus when you sense that self-judgment is rising, just acknowledge it and LET IT GO. Just release it.

Action:

The greatest pitfall in this process of realizing the truth of who we are, and the unwanted programming, which is in the way, is the mindset that we need to "fight" these processes and predilections. What happens oftentimes when we fall for this trick (which is part of the programming) is that we engage the past unwanted programming and end up strengthening it rather than getting rid of it! This happens primarily because the deep inner mind does not process "negative" focus the way we are led to believe it does and the way that we operate on the conscious levels of our mind. How is this possible? Look at the scenes in day-to-day life that are played out with our own lives and those of others – – how many times do we and others repeat the same mistakes repeatedly? Think about this not only in terms of occult practice but just in life generally.

An example is the person who is had a bad relationship. They (hopefully) remove themselves from the bad relationship with a sincere profession and desire that they will not enter such a relationship like that again. Yet, even after going through a string of bad relationships a pattern emerges. The names and faces change in the context of situations as well may change, BUT at the core the very same issues and problems arise within these relationships repeatedly. Did the person involved not want to change? They probably really did! The conscious desire, however, was overruled by the subconscious belief

Fighting the deep belief systems and programming that is possibly even below the surface of conscious awareness itself, simply does not work effectively. The subconscious mind is far more powerful than the conscious aspect of your mind and is the part of your consciousness that creates your experience of reality! In order to do anything that is effective with the subconscious aspect of your mind we need to speak the language of the subconscious mind and realize what aspects of our attempted communications are ineffective.

For example, you say consciously and with determination: "I don't want to ever do/experience/believe _____ ".

The subconscious mind hears: "**I do** want to always do/experience/believe _____ ".

As mentioned earlier the subconscious mind is not process "negative" communication. What was mentioned above is the fallacy of engaging past unwanted programming and predilections we do not like with critical self-judgment and with argumentation. How do we effectively release unwanted predilections and past programming?

FIRST, accept what is even if you do not like what you see. This is true of past programming that is rising, or certain traits characteristics and predilections that you become aware of that you do know are unhelpful. Accept what is as part of something you have created. Even if this is part of the past programming that you do not like to realize that you build upon it and edifice of your own design. Accept it. Realize that whatever the source or context, this may have served a purpose at one time that was valuable to you even if you do not understand how.

SECOND, detach yourself from the past/present programming, or unwanted traits and predilection, and in that detachment releasing any aspect of critical self-judgment.

THIRD, imagine, visualize or see the element of water within you gently washing the belief system, past programming, unwanted traits or predilections, slowly away like sand slowly gets washed away as water flows over it. Observe this without critical self-judgment, and just let it happen. When this reaches its apex (and intuitively you will know when this happens) move to step four.

FOURTH, imagine, visualize or see what you truly desire to REPLACE the unhelpful belief system, predilection or programming, slowly rising through the water within into a more and more "solid" edifice. FEEL as strongly as possible the satisfaction, joy and pleasure of this new edifice and how you love the fact that this is now part of your programming, belief pattern and thought process.

As this reaches its apex say aloud with conviction "I love that new (insert new belief, or pattern) is now part of the foundation of my growth!".

This is all a process so repeat this as often as you wish as it can only help you and will also become more and more manifest in your life with repetition.

The reason "accepting what is" remains the foundation of to change is that one cannot build anything that is not simply a warped caricature if the premise underlying the work is not accurate. Simply put, if the edifice created is based upon fantasy, the edifice itself is mere fantasy! Accepting what is no matter how painful or difficult the process is, allows us to deal with the core issues deep within that give rise to what is unhelpful and thus create on the premise of self-honesty. This process is uncomfortable in many ways because we are very adept at self-deception. This is part of the self-protective processes of our minds and is not bad but needs to be rewired through taking control of our minds back in ways mentioned previously. We need to deliberately choose self-honesty over egoic protection as the rewards far outweigh the temporary pain all the process as the pain is based upon false presumption rather than truth.

NOTES

NOTES

Chapter 2: "Dissolving Old Patterns"

After you have seriously gone through the process outlined in chapter 1, (realize you will go back to that process throughout your magical practice!) You can move into replacing old programming with what you decide is the most helpful.

You have by now identified many inner belief systems that are holding you back. Also, there has been work done to sever the emotional connections you have to those inner creations. What next?

First, is the vital work of connecting to your inner Daemon, fetch, or whatever other name you may call "it". Regardless of name, this aspect of your consciousness is a part of your deepest inner mind. To connect to your innermost mind the endless "chatter" of the egoic or "conscious" mind needs at least for periods of time to be silenced. "How can I do that?"? – You ask... It is far simpler than you may have been led to believe. This does not mean it is not challenging, but as with any habit (which is exactly what this is) after the formation time it will become as natural as breathing.

The state of inner silence is called by many names. Some call it "no mind", others call it "Zen" and still others refer to it as "non-thought". The hang-up is that the descriptions of this state of consciousness lead many to believe that this state is completely free of all forms of thought. This is damaging because it sets people up for failure and frustration at the very least! The truth is that the state of inner silence has nothing to do with not having thoughts of any kind. There would be no wisdom, connection or power from the state of consciousness if there was no thought whatsoever. What this state is ACTUALLY referring to is "thought in the universal language of imagery and emotion".

There are many layers to thought. The type of thought we are most used to you is the endless chatter of the normal waking conscious state, which is the creation of what I have called the egoic mind. We are not taught the experience of deeper thought by society, and even less in a religious thought offered to us in the modern world. Much of what is put out there is little more than contemplation or deep relaxation with no ultimate purpose other than the obvious health benefits. Many times, as well even those groups or individuals that do go deeper into conscious states never tell a person what to do when they achieve it!

To successfully navigate to the deepest inner mind, and connect with our deepest inner self, we must first learn the "language" of the mind itself that we are not taught. The second thing is the development of self-control where we can remain aware for periods of time within those deeper states so that sleep does not interfere. The language of the deepest inner mind is the same as what I discussed earlier with the language of the multiverse being intense imagery and emotion. This makes sense for as the famous occult axiom from the Emerald tablet states "as it is above, so it is below that together they may work the miracles of the one thing". We must train ourselves in this language and the most effective way that I found to do so is through deep meditational practice, affirmation within that deep meditational state, and repetition. This opens the door between the conscious and subconscious aspect of your mind allowing a more conscious flow of communication between them.

Starting out, when you go for a walk (please make sure you are not in a high-traffic area if you are in an urban center) start training yourself in entering altered states by noticing your step. Feel it as it touches the ground and be aware of the rhythm. Focus on that rhythm as you continue your walk, while still being aware of your surroundings. While you are focusing on the rhythm of your step and how it feels when your feet are contacting the surface of the ground or sidewalk, thoughts are going to arise from your egoic mind. Simply acknowledge these thoughts and let them go without engaging them in any way. Let them be as drops of water flowing off a duck's back. Continuing with this, you will find that for longer and longer periods of time the unruly thoughts will be absent and only the focus you have on the rhythm of your step and how it feels as you are walking will be there. This will not be constant but will expand in the timeframe as you do this repeatedly.

Another thing that starts to happen when you do this is that you start to enter a deeper state of consciousness. You will notice as you do this on a repetitive basis that this also expands in its timeframe. This state of consciousness is deeper than the usual state that you are in normally and is by no means the entrance to your deepest inner mind but is training your mind consciously and subconsciously along the path to bring that about.

Practicing and learning to LIVE in the connection with the deep inner mind and to shifting your consciousness from the normal state you are used to into deeper levels is vital in your quest for success in true change. This connection as it grows will always have multiple layers to it. Obviously, you will not be in the same detail in your connection when you are going about your day-to-day activities, but as this skill is being strengthened there will be an increasing awareness of the deeper levels of your being.

You may ask why it is important to be able to shift your consciousness into deeper layers and to go through any of this training at all. Mainly it is because the art of true growth and change stems from the subconscious mind, not the conscious mind. In order to facilitate change in an effective manner we must bring the conscious aspect of our thought processes, and the processes of our subconscious mind into alignment so they agree. This brings about a resonance throughout our entire being and is the catalyst of change! When we are not in that resonance, we are like a trumpet in an orchestra that is out of tune to the consternation of all listening. The unfortunate thing in our society is that this dissonance is thought of as "normal".

During and after establishing, strengthening and nurturing your ability to enter deeper levels of consciousness – and even after you have come to the realization of your deepest mind, you will want to revisit the efforts made as outlined in chapter 1 and this chapter as growth is never ending. The difference will be at that point, you will want to expand your "awareness" to more than what simply is to the potentials of what you can create.

Moving past the preliminary stages of training your mind (such as the rhythm of your step) you will want to learn how to meditate and to do so in a very deep level. When you were approach meditation seek to become aware of your body and become the observer of your thought processes. This is a lot easier than it sounds. Focusing on your breathing and allowing yourself to relax, you will find yourself entering deeper states just as you were while focusing on the rhythm of your step during walks. In fact, you will likely end up relaxing far deeper and may even fall asleep on the first few attempts, which is all right – just try again another day.

Continuing in a regular practice of meditation, make a commitment to yourself verbally if necessary, that you will be honest with yourself no matter what you may see or experience. See your own existence in what "is". Allow the little fibs we tell ourselves to boost the self-image to simply drop. This is one of the most important lessons of "accepting what is" as it brings you to the state of self-honesty to see yourself as you ARE, not what you hope or imagine yourself to be. Without this you will only spin your wheels so to speak but never move on.

In allow yourself to see yourself as you really are, warts and all keep away from self-judgment. If you slip into the critical self-judgment mentioned in chapter 1 what will happen is a strengthening of the very issue you wish to get rid of or change. When you notice yourself feeling this way when something starts to arise in your feelings while meditating, take note of it but just let it slip off you. Just gently switch your focus back to neutrality and detachment, remembering to focus on your breathing.

You will notice that the more you work in meditation with the intent to increase your awareness of self, the clearer things will become. Aspects of your life, beliefs and focus will begin to become more fleshed out. The underlying things that perhaps you are completely unaware of previously will begin to manifest themselves. This does not happen immediately, but with repetition over time and consistency and practice. When these things arise whether they are positive or negative, helpful or unhelpful, continue to hold yourself in neutrality. The reason for this is that sometimes things that even appear great may not be helpful to our evolution. In the same way some things that we may look upon in our expanding awareness that we do not like may be a part of something that is helping us grow. If we engage in critical self-judgment either in adulation or condemnation, we end up falling into the same trap of false projection.

As things begin to reveal themselves more and more, you will become more cognizant of what aspects of this self-knowledge are helpful in truth, and unhelpful. You will begin to tell the difference over time even in just the "feel" between what proceeds from the innermost mind and that which is only from the egoic mind — or what was implanted within us by others intentionally or unintentionally. That "feel" is part of our intuition and is one of the senses that as you continue engaging in this practice will become stronger and stronger. Ignore it at your own peril.

One thing that may help in this process is the creation of a personal "mantra" to be used while in the deep states of meditation.

Start by writing out your intent in a short statement or sentence which encapsulates the heart of your intent. For example, you may want to focus first on discovering who you really are and what that could subjectively mean to you. Let us say that the statement you come up with is **"see who I really am"**.

Now take away the repeated letters like this:

"sewhoirlm"

In this example it may seem that some tongue twisting word has been created! Do not be concerned about this, simply sounded out in a way that can be spoken. Here I would pronounce this word:

Phonetically: **"seh-who-I-relm"**

Please note that the last syllable is completely phonetically written and does not reflect an addition of an "E" to the mantra.

Take the personal mantra and committed to memory. The last thing you want is to be reading something while you are trying to meditate and enter deep states of consciousness — that is a tremendous distraction! When in meditation for self-discovery use this mantra as an aid along with the focus on your breathing to get away from the inner dialogue of the egoic mind, and at the same time subconsciously reinforce your intent throughout the entire meditation! This is a very powerful technique that I have used myself on many occasions and I know that it will be of great help to you. Things will arise in your awareness using something like this, that will point out areas of belief the truly hold you back in the image you hold of yourself. You will begin to see where truth lies in who you really are, and where things have been added in due to conditioning that are not necessarily even a part of your makeup. If you are doing meditation for the purpose of self-discovery which I do recommend, when things do start to become clear hold the position and focus of self-acceptance without judgment as talked about earlier. Except even those things that were imparted to you by other people, institutions both religious and secular, and well-meaning friends. These things may have been imparted to you, but you did build on them, so in a sense you do still bear responsibility for them. Realize as well that your subconscious mind is not trying to hurt you but protect you and ensure your survival.

When you become aware of things that you do since in your intuition that need to be changed, set the groundwork in your self-awareness meditations for change to occur. This would likely occur in separate meditations as you do not want to distract yourself while you are in the experience. My recommendation would be to have a journal where you will write down after your meditations are complete, what things surfaced into your awareness as a result of your intent. Perhaps make an "*" assigned the things that you sense need to be changed so that you have it fresh in your mind on your next meditation. This process is part of your magical practice and along with everything that you do magically you need to write these things in a journal especially when you are starting out on this path. This is vitally important during this process being outlined as it is the foundation of your future success! You will tell from some of the things that I write in this text that I really do believe in the power of mantras in affecting the subconscious mind.

Create a mantra based upon the intent to create change, dissolving the unhelpful beliefs/patterns that you discover in your mind. You can make it anyway you wish but you might like this example.

"I allow myself to change"

"ialowmysefdtchng"

"i-alow-mysef-teh-neg"

Phonetically spelled with creative license

Please note that you have free reign to be creative with the pronunciation of your mantras. It is the representation of the statement, not the statement itself. It will make sense to your subconscious mind!

When you are continuing in the self-awareness process entering deep meditation, as the unfolding of things within that hold you back arise switch from the first mantra to the second one just presented (or one of your own design along similar lines). As you continue to chant this new mantra, since the newfound freedom in your soul as your innermost mind begins to UNDERSTAND that you do not need to hold onto these past and present hindrances. It is important that you allow yourself to imagine, visualize or see the belief system being dissipated while as intensely as you can allowing yourself to feel emotionally the freedom that comes along with that dissipation. This invokes the universal language and as well by proxy the only language your subconscious mind truly understands.

The last stage here is to ACCEPT the changes that will occur in your experience of life spirit, mind and body as a result of these practices. This can be done by deeply, and intensely making a verbal statement to yourself (that invokes the conscious mind through the verbalization, and the subconscious mind as well by the intensity of your emotion) to this effect at the end of your meditation.

This may all seem like a lot to remember but I will recap this for you right here and you will see how simple it is. This is much more difficult to explain in written word than it is to simply speak it.

Part one:
*Get used to entering altered states by taking notice of how you walk and the rhythm of your step

Part two:
*Start the practice of meditation in addition to continuing your regular walks. Start with one mantra related to self-discovery, keeping notes in a journal as to the results. After doing this for a period of time include another mantra to be used to focus the intent of releasing unhelpful beliefs, past programming and other issues that arise in your self-awareness.

**At this stage make sure to have a closing statement of intensity affirming your desire to accept the changes this brings.*

This is something that you will cherish and use repeatedly throughout your entire magical career. There is no and to self-discovery, connection to our authentic self and the life that it brings which can be expressed throughout our entire being. This is a commitment to yourself in a way that is like no other. This will help you if you are committed and sincere to dissolve self-doubt, unhelpful indoctrination, and the common negativity that are constant bombardment in modern society brings to us every single day. Do not rush this process as you will be very happy in future practice that you allowed yourself to go through this. My experience is that this process is best served over a period of about six months. Some may find this to be less than six months and some more. Just move forward in it in a way that resonates with you. In the future this process will be continued as mentioned throughout your magical career in the same way that you like to keep your physical body clean by regular bathing.

The simple painting below shows forth the "well ordered" path of energy in the way it can be manifested to our awareness. This is NOT a restriction, rather a "channel" through which we can be UNFETTERED in our lives!

**Painted by "Kelly-Kelly",

used by permission**

NOTES

NOTES

_____

_____

_____

_____

_____

_____

_____

_____

_____

_____

_____

_____

Chapter 3: "Creating the New"

Now that you have gotten a grip on how to dissolve old patterns, you are ready to start REPLACING those patterns with helpful material! Please note that when you get a handle on creating new "programs" you will be able to COMBINE the work of this chapter with the work outlined in chapter 2.

The first thing that is needed is a clear understanding of what will be a helpful pattern to incorporate. This does not come from arbitrary desires of the egoic mind. There is a place for desire, but as a "helper" not a "mover". The will comes from the deep inner mind while the aspect of "desire" comes from the egoic mind. When these two factors work together AMAZING things can happen! When they are not, the trap of imprinting new UNHELPFUL systems exists as a very real threat.

Starting out, then, one must turn back true meditation. The purpose of meditation is to bring you to self – knowledge and self – awareness on deeper levels of consciousness than the egoic mind. The Temple at Delphi had the inscription "Know Thyself" as a reference to the mysteries of the occult. You can see once again the correlation of purpose where it comes to meditation as the foundation of all things magical at least in the realm of effective results.

Set aside a regular time (aside from any practice you are currently doing regarding cleansing old beliefs) where you can have at least fifteen minutes of undisturbed silence.

Begin meditating with the intent of learning the "will" of your innermost mind (or inner Daemon if you will). You may want to create a mantra encapsulating your intent, but it is not necessary unless you feel that it is.

Practicing this short meditation, you will want to have a pen and a notebook with you. It does not matter if you receive some sort of "flash of insight", although sometimes you may, during this meditation. The purpose is to lower the barrier that exists between the conscious and subconscious mind. Meditation, if you allow it will do this very effectively!

When the meditation is complete, before you leave make sure to write down in the notebook whatever comes to your mind and awareness. Do NOT think about what you will write down – just WRITE it! The moment you think about what you were going to write, you are engaging the egoic mind and will warp what you write to unimaginable degrees.

You may find that in this process you write several things, not just one thing. Afterwards, when you look at what you wrote it may even seem "nonsense" to your awareness. Do not be concerned about this, just leave it with no alteration.

Do this little meditation for two weeks, keeping the notebook up to date with everything you write down. When the two weeks of past, you can then begin to interpret what has been written with the full engagement of your egoic mind. This is done in a specific manner which I am about outline.

OUTLINE FOR CREATION/REPROGRAMMING

When you have immersed yourself in the practice as mentioned above for two weeks begin in this meditation to add the following after you have written down a condensed interpretation to your current level of understanding of what you wrote in the previous two weeks.

The Touchstone

In your meditation starting at the third week, when you are in as much of a state of "inner silence" as you can manage, begin to visualize or create in your imagination, your own form physically expanding in size. In the way most effective for you, see yourself "growing" with every in breath dwarfing first the earth; the solar system; your concept of the universe. Create in your imagination this expansion as though you were incorporating everything within you rather than being superimposed over the imagery.

Continue in this expansion in your mind's eye. Let the expansion continue with every in breath. When you have reached what you feel to be the apex of this expansion allow yourself a moment of pause.

After taking this moment upon us, allow yourself to change in form and become indistinct, like a shapeless "envelope" encompassing ALL THINGS.

At this point just hold the visualization mentioned above inasmuch inner silence as you were able. If you find your thoughts wondering that is okay – just gently bring yourself back to the inner silence. The time you can hold that inner silence will increase over time and with practice.

While holding the state of consciousness allow yourself awareness to open further without restraint. Just let it happen! There is nothing you need to do except allow it to be. You may end of hearing sounds, or perhaps see flashes of imagery while doing this. Realize that that is a distraction at this point from your egoic mind. Eventually and with repeated practice you will begin to sense a very quiet, powerful presence that cannot be grasped or visualized but is intuitively there. This is what you are looking for! Just allow this awareness to be even if but for a moment as this presence is your inner Daemon or as I often say your "authentic self". Just touch on this unless you are already deeply familiar with this presence as the focus here is not union with the Daemon (that will come later). At this point in your practice the awareness and EXPERIENCE of this presence is enough, and you can remember this feeling and call it forth now in all your future practice!

Dissolution

Now after step one has been done to satisfaction the meditation can shift. Realize that this is going to take you time and that rushing this entire process will only harm your efforts. If it takes you a period to master step one in the expansion of this meditation let it be. When you are ready you will be able to move on to this step and just incorporate everything in this process until it is complete.

You have from the previous chapter, reframed many unhelpful belief systems without engaging them in self-defeating ways. Now it is time to change the underlying energetic current that has provided fertile soil for these unhelpful systems to grow in us.

When you are at the apex of your meditation INVOKE silently, through memory the feeling of the presence of the inner Daemon you experienced in step one. Realize that this presence is your unborn, authentic self – who you TRULY are!

While in this state give a "body" to your will by saying with the authority of the fact presence: "it is my will to experience (insert the helpful belief that you wish to use to counter the unhelpful belief you have been reframing)

Hope the intent that you have embodied with these words as strongly as possible, FEELING it in your spirit mind and body. This is very important because you must engage the spirit the mind and the body or it will not be as effective as it could be. Simply allow what was unhelpful before to slip completely out of your focus as you are choosing to empower what you have just stated as your will. Just let the old ways go – it really is as simple as that.
Close out of your meditation and work.

You can see how this builds upon the work of chapter 2 in a progressive manner. Feel free to return to this process often as it completely entrenches with the power of your inner Daemon those things that bring you towards effective growth.

If you find in the future that some unhelpful systems of belief that are limiting you in your growth raise their head (as oftentimes the deep roots of some indoctrinated beliefs raise their head in a progression as we continue to uncover things within our subconscious mind) just returned to this process as you can continue to use this to reprogram your mind – taking control of your thoughts and your mind back on an ongoing basis throughout your entire life.

NOTES

_____

_____

_____

_____

_____

_____

_____

_____

_____

_____

_____

_____

_____

_____

NOTES

CHAPTER 4: "The Premise of Change"

It is vitally important for you to remember not to underestimate the work in the previous chapters! Much of the success that you may have depends upon how you condition yourself in the preparations and prerequisites. Many people who write on the subjects, lecture or talk at other formats, do not take the time to explain how important it is for you to hone the most important tool in your entire arsenal – you yourself!

One of the biggest reasons if not the biggest reason that you need to focus on cleansing yourself from past belief systems, is the fact that we have all been programmed from birth through many different sources. This is not something that anyone of us has escaped, and it colors our view of the world, ourselves and the universe like colored glasses. Failure to deal with these issues and to put ourselves on the proper footing for effectiveness is one of the biggest reasons why people either end up frustrated on the occult path or even go as far as blowing up their lives! We cannot be like ostriches with our heads in the sand when it comes to this.

The key to understanding the premise and the actual process that has been described previously is what I have belabored regarding self-honesty. What do I mean by self-honesty? The biggest part of self-honesty is admitting that we have indeed been mentally programmed! For some reason many people have a hard time with this admission. It is as though they feel they are insulting themselves by admitting that their minds have been molded and shaped according to someone else's agenda. This resistance serves to reinforce the mental programming that is there (and yes you have it! So do I, and everyone else). The way to deal with this is to take a step back from the emotional attachment to the very question itself about whether we have been mentally programmed. In this state of detachment, consider your childhood. What influence did your parents have on you? What about your friends when you were going to school? What kinds of things did they teach you in school? As you grew older, perhaps you went to university. What kind of things did they begin to impress upon you there? Were they useful things? Some of them certainly were I am sure! There were also many things that were taught according to a viewpoint that looks upon you as a human being as a commodity to consumerist philosophy. Perhaps if you are of a religious sort, you were impressed that you were to be the servant of a supreme deity.

This indoctrination and mental programming were not done as a malicious act by anyone, save perhaps those that have bombarded us to this day with entertainment and advertisement specifically designed to create in the and covetousness for the materialistic world. Most of the mental programming that you and I received was done out of a sense of responsibility to help us cope with the way the world "works" so that we could make something of ourselves financially and socially. This is not "wrong" as we do need to have these concepts in order to make headway in the world of limitation from our perceptive experience. It becomes wrong when we are enslaved by the idea that these concepts are ultimate truth and represent the sum and total of what and who we are. As a society does not generally accept what is beyond the realm of the five senses and the perception of the physical body as being "real" the mental programming often does take that bent of excluding all other things from the picture thus enslaving us in spirit mind and body.

The purpose of the first chapter in this book was to begin recognizing and becoming aware of what exists within our current mental programming (at that stage) and what kind of hold it has on us. To see things as they are is as mentioned earlier assuming an emotionally detached position to analyze what things become apparent within our awareness during that aspect of our process. This is not so that we can begin fighting ourselves by feeling shame, regret, frustration and all the like. This is the main reason for the emotional detachment which can be achieved even if but for short time depending on whether you are a calm or passionate person by nature.

In this state of emotional attachment when we begin to perceive what is actually there in our belief systems, rather than taking energy to fight and attempt in futility to change this mental programming by force, we ACCEPT that we have believed these things whatever they may be in specific focus. As I mentioned earlier in this chapter much of this mental programming was not done maliciously! There was a purpose behind most of it whether it was from educational institutions, parents, peers, religious and societal constructs. Accepting that we have been mentally programmed simply takes the fight away from the experience so that we can put the energy towards real change instead of the frustration and futility of dividing against ourselves. Let me tell you something very clearly: if you have a fight with your subconscious mind you will never ever win. Accepting what "is", is the first step in self honesty and in the premise of what has been talked about before. During the first chapters work and exercise you will notice many different things coming into your awareness and some of them may be very shocking to you as the things we have been programmed with go on deep levels of our subconscious mind. What we are aware of consciously is only the "tip of the iceberg" where it comes to the things we have accepted which hold us back. Please do not be discouraged by this truth as we have all been there and it is something that can be worked out – just not through fighting ourselves internally.

When we have accepted what is, we are able then to disempower the programming in a progressive manner as deeper and deeper aspects of that programming continue to come into our awareness. Realize that this is a lifelong process and not something you do in a month!! After nearly 40 years of occult practice I still go back and work on things that are within the depths of my subconscious mind.

To disempower these aspects of mental programming the first thing to be done after accepting it is to be grateful for the fact that your subconscious mind embedded this programming with the intent to help you. Taking the attitude of "self-judgment", plays into knee-jerk emotional reactions which take away from the detachment that is necessary, and help you to sink deeper into the very mental programming you're working to release in the same way that a struggling victim within a pit of quicksand will sink faster if they flail about. Accept what you have become aware of and then be grateful for the fact that your subconscious mind was attempting to incorporate in trust something it thought would be helpful to your growth.

When you have done this, you will be moving into what was talked about in chapter 2 where you dissolve the power of the mental programming. This is much easier than you would think if you have successfully accepted and expressed to your inner self gratitude even though you really do not want to be bound by the mental programming you become aware of any longer. In this spirit and attitude you have already cultivated, within the deep meditative states you are becoming familiar with getting into in chapter 2, begin to build the emotional sense of neutrality. What away mean by that? It means that after you have accepted and expressed to your inner self gratitude, allow your emotional state to fall away from you in the same way as other things will mentally as you enter deep meditative consciousness. You do not want to express power towards the unwanted mental programming. This is important for what is going to be discussed in the next chapter which is about anchoring and reframing your consciousness and is something to be understood alongside chapter 3.

You will want to have something that you begin to associate as an image either as a creation in your imagination, or perhaps the memory of an event that can represent the undesired mental programming. You will want to associate this image in your mind with it in the same way that you would associate a thumbnail icon with a friend on social media. Remember that imagery and feeling are part of the universal language that your subconscious mind understands very clearly and is the natural mode of its communication. Perhaps you will want to draw a representation in your journal and use that as a focal point for the imagery. However you decide to do so it is important that you have an image that you can bring into your mind either through your imagination or through visualization of some sort.

To recap what I have been talking about in this chapter I will give you a list that you can write in your journal if you so desire. You may want to have this is you revisit chapters 1 and 2.

1.)   As undesired mental programming manifests in your   awareness, ACCEPT

2.)   Allow yourself to experience   GRATITUDE

3.)   Go into deep meditation and release any emotional connection good or bad to the mental programming

4.)   Visualize or create in your imagination and image to be connected to the mental programming

When you have moved through chapters 1 and 2 using what I have been mentioning in this chapter, you will be ready to move into chapter 3 and the information in the following chapter which is a companion to it.

NOTES

NOTES

_____

_____

_____

_____

_____

_____

_____

_____

_____

_____

_____

_____

_____

Chapter 5: Anchoring and Reframing

This chapter is to go in conjunction with chapters 2 and 3 as a companion even as chapter 4 was to be a companion to chapter 1.

I know that this particular chapter is going to be of great interest to you because it's something that is very practical, and will elucidate the reasons behind the procedures outlined in chapters 2 and 3 for creating new systems that are helpful to you in your growth. You can bring the things talked about in this chapter into practical use in your everyday life and develop yourself magically as well so that when you are working in meditation or ritual work you may be able to experience the maximum effectiveness possible. This is a much more modern slant than what you may be used to in books that talk about occultism and magick, but it is necessary to use the tools that we have in our modern day to bring the wisdom and knowledge of ancient practice into the 21st-century so that it is relevant to us in all aspects.

The concepts of anchoring and reframing that I am going to be talking about in this chapter are also valuable beyond being a companion to the 2nd and 3rd chapters of this book. Anchoring and reframing aspects of your consciousness also has limitless usefulness in your meditational practice, in your magical practice both private and in a group, and in your day-to-day life as you face the challenges that come to us all where it comes to real growth. Some of the material I am talking about in this chapter can also be seen in video format in a broadcast that was put out in 2018 on our YouTube channel and it is appropriately named *"Anchoring and Reframing Consciousness"*. You can find the link URL for that video among many others in the bibliography at the end of this book.

One of the things that learning how to anchor and reframe consciousness effectively does is sharpen our abilities when we are looking inward (as talked about in chapter 1 in far more detail) so that we can tell the difference between the mutterings of our "egoic mind" and that which proceeds from the shadowy self and the intuitive impulses of the inner Daemon. Please do not underestimate the importance of all this prerequisite work as to do so will in my experience, anyway, hinder you in effectiveness and true power in ways that will set you back many years in your practice.

Transformation, expansion and growth is a never-ending process. The moment that growth stops death occurs! Death is not actually the cessation of existence as energy is neither created nor destroyed. Death is a stagnation of spirit mind and body and it starts in the spirit, moves through into the mind and finally into the body like a miserable cancer that eats away at you. "Resurrection" is not some mystified state, as most of us in the entirety of the human race have been in a state of spiritual "death" that has moved on into so many different aspects of the spirit mind and body due to the past programming that we had. By **choosing deliberately** to obliterate the past programming that has caused this state of "death", we reanimate and reverse that process. This does not mean that physically we will not die as our physical bodies begin to deteriorate towards death as we understand it in the world of limitation from the moment we are born. What it does mean is that we may be able to experience "immortality" in the sense that that everlasting expansion and growth becomes ingrained as the primary programming of our existence strengthened by our deliberate choice!! The difference to be put in terms of our understanding here, would be looking at a beautiful flowing river filled with life and ecosystems thriving, compared to a Farmer's slew that is stagnant and stinks! Within the bounds of the illustration given, which would you prefer in terms of your existence?

There is a price to be paid for everything that we do either in the physical world or in spiritual effort. This is something I want to make sure that you understand because there are many out there that believe that everything should be "free". While this is true in terms of the arbitrary economics of the world of limitation in which we live, there is always a movement with frequency, or vibration, or energy whatever you wish to call it. This is best shown by the way the weather patterns move across the earth. The reason that we experience gentle breezes, horrific tornadoes, gentle rain or hailstorms, is because of the cycles that take place within nature itself. Heat evaporates the water which then cools often turns into clouds. Within the clouds the water particles mixed with dust in turn into droplets that fall to the earth as rain – the water is returned. The breezes and the winds take place because there are imbalances within the atmosphere throughout our earth and the atmospheric flow is always seeking in vain to balance everything. There is always in exchange taking place in nature. This is true as well among the stars, as even they do not last forever. Out of their "death" new stars can be formed. The stars including our own son have what is called a "solar wind" which is part of the radiation particles that are flowing out from it. There is an effect that is experienced by different bodies when they are exposed to that solar wind. Therefore, comets appear to have a tail when they pass by in our observable – the tail is caused by the solar wind and points away from the sun no matter which direction the comet is moving. These are just natural phenomenon that shows some of the aspects of energetic exchange. This is no different when it comes to us personally! There is a price to be paid for spiritual growth and do not ever believe anyone who tells you there is not. The price however is something that is worth the sacrifice. You are "paying" by sacrificing those things which are illusions for that which is true. As we cannot define the infinite, this "truth" cannot be understood in its fullness either by anyone but can be grasped in elementary essence. It is this "truth" that drives us forward to endless expansion and endless growth for we grow infinitely and yet are still never finished.

It is amazing to me even though I was also in that boat myself many times, that people treasure the illusion to such a degree that they are not willing to sacrifice it. There is the fear of loss which binds one to the world of limitation like no other force. I will tell you that the loss is not a loss at all – – you never really had it to begin with. What you are doing in truth is treating in what is not real for that which has lasting power. The fear of loss is generated by the egoic mind because it fears deeply that it will become irrelevant to you and it is used to being the "Lord of the house" by the binding to limitation that we experience through the programming we have received. What happens is that the egoic mind goes back into its proper place as the interpreter of the impulses of the inner Daemon. This accentuates the importance of the egoic mind but in its proper order. You may want to do a series of meditations that you design yourself on this very concept.

Now, in your practices in chapter 3 especially (you can start with the practices in chapter 2 as well to get familiar with how this works) you will need to take what was talked about in the companion chapter 4 chapter 1 in regards to the emotional imagery that you created for the unhelpful belief system. Now realize as well in a talk about belief systems I am talking about any and all types of inner programming that go against growth. It could be small it could be large and complex.

In chapter 4 you created a symbol of imagery that you emotionally connected to the unhelpful belief system. You practiced holding that in intensity and then releasing the emotional connection. Now you are going to understand why this was important as what is necessary is for you to uncover what the progressive and helpful programming for growth is that you wish to use to replace this unhelpful programming. As mentioned earlier in this chapter there is always an energetic exchange. You are in this process paying the price so to speak by sacrificing the unhelpful programming for that which is instead is based upon the impulses of your inner Daemon. If you have uncertainty go back to chapters 2 and 3 and re-read them carefully. Make sure that you have been doing the practices that were mentioned in outlined within those chapters.

As you are now in the process of creating a new "program" for your subconscious and conscious mind to agree upon together, you will want to take the new belief or program and symbolize it in the same way that you did with the unhelpful belief or program previously. Spend as much time building this up as you did on the unhelpful belief system or program. This is very important because you are going to be taking away the one program which is going to leave a "vacuum" that needs to be immediately filled within your deep inner mind. If you have nothing to replace what you are taking away, the old program will reassert itself by default. This is something that is often overlooked when people are talking about real change – – they are quite adept at identifying problems but are not clear in how to replace what has been a hindrance with something new. Let us not make that mistake here!

When you are at the stage of dissolving the old belief systems talked about and outlined in chapter 3, you will want to incorporate the following into the meditation/personal change work.

When you are visualizing, creating in your imagination the unhelpful belief system as outlined in chapter 3, change the way that you have been "seeing" this to be the symbol you have been working on in chapter 4 to represent the unhelpful belief system. Allow yourself to feel the intensity of the emotional connection. Remember to feel the gratitude for the fact that your inner mind has been trying to help you even though it was not effective. Hold this within your inner mind for as long as possible. When you feel the apex has been reached (and you will know) **allow yourself** to release the emotional connection. Just let it go! If you overthink it the process will become very difficult – just do it without thinking.

When you feel that you have sufficiently detached yourself emotionally from the connection to the symbol of the unwanted programming, focus on the symbol that you have been creating for that which is helpful programming. Imagine, or create in your imagination that symbol and all that it represents to you feeling emotional connection to it as intensely as possible. It is quite all right to work yourself up into that emotional state! This is not about being "fake" it is about using your emotions as a tool. This will be useful to you later in practical magical operations. The emotions you need to feel are pleasure, joy, gratitude – the emotions involved with determination are not important here. Pleasure joy and gratitude are very powerful movers to the subconscious mind and communicate a message that this is what you **truly want** and that is what you are working for in change involving your innermost or subconscious mind.

What I am about to say now is extremely **important**. When you reach the apex of the emotional intensity, make a gesture even if it is as simple as touching your forefinger to your thumb. What you were doing here is within that emotional and symbolic imagery connecting a physical action to this state that you are feeling right now amid the intensity.

When you have done this complete with the gesture, release the creation in your visualization or imagination. Call back the imagery and emotion of the unwanted mental programming once again and repeat this process. Continue to repeat this process going from the unwanted belief system to the new programming you wish to incorporate. Doesn't this reinforce the unwanted programming? **Actually no!** What you are doing is communicating through the universal language of imagery and emotion to your innermost or subconscious mind that you wish **to replace** the unwanted programming with the new program you have instituted. Repeat this process that has been described 10 times in a row. By doing it 10 times in a row you are reinforcing the message that you are sending to your subconscious mind and reinforcing the gesture that you have chosen to make as a **trigger** for the state of joy, pleasure, and gratitude. This will be apparent in its reasons very shortly.

You will want to go through this process with the meditations specifically outlined in chapter 3 for a full month. Yes, this is a commitment in time and practice, but it is vitally important because I do know is you read this book you want to learn how to be an effective and powerful magician. This is part of the price that is necessary if you want the real thing.

To recap what has been mentioned and outlined in this chapter I have put the following for your convenience:

Steps for Anchoring and Reframing

1. Follow through with the practice in meditation outlined in chapter 3
2. FOCUS on the symbol of the unwanted programming along with its emotional connections
3. When at the apex, release and detach yourself emotionally from the symbol of the unwanted programming
4. When this detachment is established replace it with the symbol of the programming you wish to incorporate along with all its emotional attachment
5. At the apex of this experience make a gesture (such as touching your forefinger to your thumb) and hold the emotional state of pleasure, joy and gratitude as intensely as possible
6. Repeat this process from the beginning (excluding the beginning of the meditation in chapter 3 – the repetition is for this process only) 10 times in a row

When you have gone through this process for 30 days you will have successfully and permanently changed a deep inner program that you have found in your practices of self-awareness has been a hindrance to your growth. In sacrificing that you have replaced it fulfilling the energetic exchange, with programming that you have discovered will be helpful for you in all areas of your life. You will want to go through the 1st five chapters of this book not only in preparation for what is to follow here but for the rest of your magical career in the process of Ascension itself.

NOTES

_____

_____

_____

_____

_____

_____

_____

_____

_____

_____

_____

_____

_____

_____

NOTES

_____

_____

_____

_____

_____

_____

_____

_____

_____

_____

_____

_____

_____

Chapter 6: The Segway

You will realize as you have been going through the chapters of this book that this is a process that will take you time. It is very important for you to set aside regular time for yourself in laying the foundation for your growth and your Ascension ultimately. Failure to do this is extremely detrimental and I cannot emphasize that enough. I do understand that there is excitement and a desire to skip ahead and get to the "good stuff" and yet what is to follow in this book has the potential to on the one hand, be a complete failure in effectiveness for you or even worse, begin a process that unravels your mind if you do not take the time to invest in yourself so that your foundation is strong.

Magick is not something that is an activity that you do on a certain day of the week. Magick in the context of this book is something that makes up the very fabric of who you are! EVERYTHING, even those things in our day-to-day life are to be part of magickal practice. The only difference between what happens in our day-to-day life and what happens in "official" magickal practice is the increased focus on the deliberate nature of how you desire to manifest your will. Most of us before the practice of magick, were unaware of the many laws of the universe that work through the energy of the infinite to create what we consider reality in our perception. The entire process was done by default subconsciously and we called it "fate". In coming to understand the practice of magick itself, we have seen that this entire process of manifestation on all levels of existence can be done DELIBERATELY rather than by default. Our effectiveness in this entire process is based upon what we have BECOME. The power that one has is not based upon how a ritual is performed, or whether the words that are there are spoken correctly, rather it is the strength of the connection one has to their inner Daemon and how much of the infinite power of what is beyond the veil one can channel through them in focus combined with will.

Perhaps you may want to reread the previous paragraph. You see, the inner Daemon is connected to in the deepest inner mind which is the subconscious. In order to have the ability to create change in accordance with will one must be able to flow in unity with the subconscious/inner Daemon. Chapters one through five have gone through ways to connect with that aspect of yourself and reprogram inhibiting and limiting belief systems so that you can flow more and more harmoniously in the connection you forge with that aspect of yourself. The importance of this is obvious.

Unless you happened to be born into wealth, you will have had or currently have employment to work in day-to-day life for the purpose of gaining money. This is an obvious necessity as things cost money. You will spend forty hours a week perhaps or more depending on what you do, exchanging time in your life for this currency with which you pay for the bills you incur to live in our society. How many hours do you think that works out to in the course of your entire lifetime? Is it too much to ask of yourself, to set aside sixty minutes in the course of the day to build yourself into something eternal?

My little sermon is done, but I do hope amid this that you do really take the time to go through the first five chapters of this book and practice what is in there for your own betterment. I would recommend that you do this consistently for six months before

Moving into the practices of the practical section of this book apart from the first ritual that is recorded. This is not unreasonable in terms of building yourself for effectiveness and success on this path.

There are also many tools that have been produced that can help you in all these processes that will have URLs placed at the back of this book.

The next section of this book is going to be dealing with rituals practices that you can start to work on in practical manifestation. I am going to be starting with what affects you spiritually, moving on into workings that affect you in your mind and then finally with works that you can do physically for the purpose of manifestation within your experience of reality.

Success and power to you as you sincerely and with self-honesty work towards your Ascension!

NOTES

_____

_____

_____

_____

_____

_____

_____

_____

_____

_____

_____

_____

_____

NOTES

_____

_____

_____

_____

_____

_____

_____

_____

_____

_____

_____

_____

_____

Part II: Practical Magick

Chapter 7: "Centering Your Self"

Now that we are moving into more practical operation in the magickal path it is important to start out from the place where you can be "grounded" within the stability however illusory that you have created for yourself by the prerequisites for magickal success. The ritual below alone is the one that you can practice during the process in the earlier parts of this book as it will not interfere with the process of reprogramming your mind. This is an important phase and I know that it may be difficult to do because you have excitement, and truly desire to move ahead with the "good stuff" but moving into that area prematurely can invoke the egoic mind and completely undermine everything that you're trying to do for long-lasting effectiveness.

The following ritual was channeled by a demonic king who goes by many names. Asmodeus, Aeshma, Eshm, Asmodi, and so on. This spirit is a great King and a very ancient spirit despite his appearance in the medieval grimoires.

What I was told when this ritual was given to me, was that it was completely un-offensive to the demonized spirits of "darkness" and basically gave them a call to let them know you desire to have your personal space. Where the egregores of the false light are concerned, it casts them out of your sphere of experience for a period with the same left foot "kick" as a full-on exorcism where they are concerned!

It would be my advice to perform this ritual at least once per day until you have it completely memorized and can do it as naturally as breathing. Do not worry about being able to "see" the visualizations, it is enough for you to "imagine" that these things are there and to KNOW that it is all there. I emphasize this because belief is the sister of doubt. Do not believe that these things are there in any visualization that you are asked to do as that is the precursor of failure. KNOW they are there with absolute certainty by an act of your will. Perhaps you have no issue with visualization and think that that is not a matter that you need to worry about, but with your skill in being able to visualize things it is important to have that deep conviction just as strongly as someone who has issues with visualization.

With that said let us see the ritual, you have permission to photocopy this or to write it out for your own use.

Centering/Banishing Ritual

This ritual was Channeled by the spirit Aeshma

Imagine yourself growing, to fill ALL the cosmos, galaxies and all to the best of your ability—do not stress, just ALLOW the visualization to grow.

Imagine a thin, translucent veil around the edges of the cosmos you visualize, imagine, see or feel. Beyond this veil, is INFINITY, darkness.

Imagine a "black hole" above you and below you, tearing through the imagined fabric of this veil.

Raise your left-hand index finger forward, pointing

straight above you into the black hole above your head.

Imagine a stream of black light (when you are more advanced imagine a stream of thick, black flame) descending to touch your finger.

Draw it down, then imagine this black light or black flame filling your main chakras one by one, until by the time your left hand is pointing down to your feet--at the 2nd black hole spinning there. The chakras are filled with this black light/flame. Imagine visualize or see the chakras glowing black, with a deep indigo outline.

Chakras from the top down:

1) Crown: Sahasrara
2) Third Eye: Ajna
3) Throat: Vishudda
4) Heart: Anahata
5) Solar Plexus: Manipura
6) Sacral: Svadhishthana
7) Root: Muladhara

This point with your left hand down and finger pointing towards your feet, imagine the chakras shattering and becoming a single field of force that is completely made of black fire.

At this point: say "from my True Self to myself, I SHATTER all limitation!"

Now, raise your left hand, index finger still pointing, until it is straight out in front of you. Imagine black light or fire rushing out from your entire being consuming all things infinitely before you.

Say: "before me is eternal darkness."

(For subsequent directions say "behind me..."; "to my right..."; "to my left" etc.)

Repeat the same way, altering the direction you are pointing accordingly. For BEHIND you simply point with your left hand (index finger extended) *as far behind your back as you can comfortably reach.* In this order:

1.) In front first
2.) Behind second
3.) Right side
4.) Left side last

Now put your hand in this mudra (see picture) in front of your heart center and say: "**I give myself to myself! United black fire of Spirit we are ONE!**"

*Relax and simply let the visualization fade it is done.

Demonic spirits are not offended by this kind of banishing/centering ritual. In fact, they will simply respect give you your space. Any false egregores will be cast out of your presence! You will find with the use of this ritual that you will increase the strength of your connection to your innermost being. A direct quote in this experience from Aeshma:

"*This also unites the 7 powers into a single field of force that can only but shatter limitation!*"

Hand Mudra:

NOTES

NOTES

Chapter 8: "Ritual Structure"

The first thing that is important to do especially when you are starting out on this path, is have a plan. When you have reached the time where you are rather advanced in your practice you are able to move forward even if it is "off-the-cuff" because the experience you have a is what I'm going to talk about to be automatic. Having a plan is important in just about every aspect of life where you are creating something and magick is no exception.

There are many ways that you can effectively organize yourself for successful magical practice, and I do not want you to think for a moment that what I am sharing here is some sort of dogmatic rule. All that I ask is that you take the time to go through the structure that I am going to show you until you become familiar with the principles. Once you are familiar with how things work and why you will be able to design your own type of structure/plan that is completely suited to the way you like to do things without losing the integrity of the principles involved.

The first thing that you need to do is long before the ritual is enacted. You need to settle on your INTENT, and the reason you are wanting to perform the magick in mind. The intent of your working is extremely important, and I would venture to say as important as the strength of your will. If you are ineffective with your intent it is going to mean that you are ineffective with your will and the entire operation will be only a bad playacting experience. This means that you are going to need to harness the power of your emotions. This is very important as well later as I will be explaining, as your emotional engagement is one of the things that opens the door into what is anchored within your subconscious mind. Memories are actually "memorable" because there is an emotion attached to them hence, we can recall them with little difficulty. Those things that we have done or experience that do not have this emotional engagement are far more difficult to remember. This is just how our minds work.

Now, in mentioning the importance of emotion I do NOT want you to think for a moment that you need to be an overly emotional person to be successful in magick. This conversely does not mean that if you are a very passionate person that you are going to have success in everything that you do magickally. What I am saying is that it is an important trigger that opens the channel to what is anchored within your subconscious mind. This entails a measure of control or comes to your emotions. I am not talking about suppression or repression of emotional states is that can be very unhealthy for us as human beings. What I am talking about is understanding the difference between being led by our emotions (which can be a truly disconcerting trip down the garden path in most experiences in life) and being able to use emotions as a "tool".

In using emotions as a tool, you are not disempowering emotion in your life. Rather you are using the techniques that you have learned earlier in this book, to enter into a neutral state when you are either meditating or performing magick, using the emotions that you possess as conduits from that neutral position to reach into the depths of your innermost being. You will see why this is important and what I mean by this if you are confused this point, as I am going to be going through this within this chapter as well is in the next chapter where I talk about how to send magick to its target.

Once you have worked on your intent and you are very clear on what and why you are doing the magickal operation being planned, begin the process of preparation for the working by incorporating the feelings that you are experiencing with your intent into your meditational practices. What you want to really focus on building at this stage is an increase in your "longing" for the desired result of your magickal work. You may find this also helps you in your motivation for getting everything else prepared, including the implements that you may wish to use if any, and the space that you wish to do the magickal work in.

There is no set time on what your preparation should be, but do not rush this phase. Intuitively you will have a sense of "release" when you have prepared long enough for this working to be effective. Rushing through this will only give you a sense of failure before your results even have a chance to be created.

Next, when you are at the time when your magickal work is to be done, make sure that you set aside about thirty minutes prior to the actual enactment of your ritual for a period of meditation to get your mind into this state necessary to be in connection with the astral plane and your intent equally at the same time.

This is not a division of your will; it is an alteration of your consciousness from the normal waking state into the deep alpha state (when you are beginning in this work) or the light Theta state as you become more advanced. It is important for this to be accomplished before doing the ritual work itself because all magick is accomplished astrally not through the power of the waking state. Once you have felt that you are within a mild to deep altered state of consciousness yet still able to communicate with your physical environment, you are ready to rise and go to your ritual "proper".

Doing the ritual itself now you need to bear in mind and bring back to mind your intent and the emotion that goes along with it. This is important whether you are creating a talisman, amulet, or evoking/invoking a spirit as you are engaging multiple aspects of your soul complex and psychological makeup towards a single goal.

Do not rush this at all! Allow the emotional connection to your intent to build and when you find yourself at the apex of how much emotional energy you can hold to your intent, change the emotion from an intense "longing" to a sense of the results having ALREADY HAPPENED! Think of how you would feel with your desire, intent, and will within your possession or within your experience already. Do you feel gratitude? Do you feel pleasure? Do you feel fulfillment? These are the types of questions that can help you locate the type of emotional response you are transforming the original emotional state into doing the ritual. When you feel that building to the same intensity as the intense longing you started out with, hold it for as long as possible while you gaze at the sigil, the talismanic object or whatever else is the subject that you are using in the ritual. While you are holding this emotional intensity locked into your intent, keep the inner narrator out of the picture by focusing any additional attention (you would be surprised how much we have despair for the inner narrator's intrusions!) On the rhythm of your breath.

When the proper point arrives which you will intuitively know, you are now at the climax of the ritual. Take a very deep breath filling your lungs entirely, and then release your intent and your emotion on your out breath, seeing it blow through the depths of the universe itself. When you have done this, you have reached the closing of the ritual. Make a brief statement of thanks and gratitude for the results you are getting and conversely if you have been dealing with the spirit thank the spirit for having spent time with you. If you like at this point you may perform the "Centering/Banishing Ritual" or do something that resonates with you that gives an indication to your entire mind that your magickal ritual is now over.

This is where it is important for you not to be controlled entirely by your emotions. The ritual is now complete and now it is vitally important for you to leave the area and do something completely different to distract yourself from thinking in any way about what you have done. This does not mean that thoughts will not stray, and you will think about the ritual. We are human beings and guess what when we know we are not supposed to do something, we always end up thinking about it are doing it! Rather than giving it energy when that happens though, when you think of what you have done magically just remember briefly the emotional state that you were in when you were imagining what you felt having all the things that you were intending in the magickal operation. When you do that than just bring your mind back to whatever other things you are doing.

This is a similar procedure to what I was talking about in the first part of this book when I was describing "non-thought". Do not engage yourself as though you are a combatant with yourself as that always ends in failure. Just be thankful and bring your mind back away from those thoughts to what you would be doing whether it is watching a movie, reading a book, visiting with friends – something completely non-magickal.

To recap I am going to show you an outline that incorporates what I have just talked about. You have permission to draw this out or to photocopy it, scan it or what have you for your own personal use.

1.) Settle on Your Intent

Make sure you know the What Where and Why of your magical operation, and how you feel about what you desire.

2.) Pre-Ritual Meditation

Take at least 30 minutes prior to performing your actual ritual to use the tool of meditation to enter an altered state of consciousness. This is vital to the effectiveness of your work!

3.) Engage Your Entire Mind, Conscious and Subconscious

As you begin the work within your ritual make sure that you focus with all your might on your intent and allow the emotions you have been building in your pre-ritual work to become fever pitch.

4.) Shift Your Emotional State to the Past Tense

At the apex of your emotional state shift your feelings from longing to fulfillment. this is extremely important!

5.) Close Your Ritual with Gratitude

Make sure if you have worked with spirits to thank them for their attendance. In other ways and another works make sure to allow yourself to experience gratitude for the fulfillment of your magick.

6.) Take Your Attention Completely Away from All Things Magickal

Do something completely different and just allow what you have done to run its course or conversely if you have been working with spirits, just let them do their work without your unintended "assistance". If you happen to think of the ritual and what you did just remember what you felt when you sent that magick forth and then bring your attention completely back to the tasks or activities you are doing currently.

In the next chapter I am going to go into far more detail with the way your emotional state affects your magickal work. Many people have talked about rituals, working with spirits and provided all kinds of grimoires but have not in many instances talked about the kind of state psychologically a person needs to be in for successful operations involving any of the above.

The next chapter is going to be exciting and useful in every magickal work that you do!

NOTES

NOTES

Chapter 9: "Sending Magick"

In the previous chapter we talked about the structure of rituals and how the flow is important in order to keep your focus intact. In this chapter I am going to be talking about the climax of the ritual itself which is the "sending" of the intent which is been charged with your focus towards its intended target/purpose.

The process is simple to explain but more challenging to do when you are first starting out in these practices. In the same way that you must prepare the structure of the ritual with care, the effectiveness of what you are doing depends on this entire process through to the climax of your working being interwoven into your very person.

From the time that you are formulating your intent in the process of creating your ritual in its different facets, you need to take that time to process your "why" and anchor it deeply into your emotional state. This is where your emotions are tremendous for your success and effectiveness! In the preparatory stages remind yourself of your intent and allow yourself to feel an intense longing for the result of the magick you are going to do. Especially during the time leading up to the ritual (whether it be days or weeks) allow yourself to experience this desire and longing upon your arising from bed, and when you retire for the evening.

When you are at the time of the ritual itself, during your pre-ritual meditation allow these emotions that you have been feeling in your longing and desire to reach a fever pitch. During this time as well, allow yourself to start feeling somewhat sexually aroused. Allow your desire and longing for the intended result to become like fever pitch lust as you would just prior to the act of sexual intercourse. Do not be concerned about the physical effects of this aspect of the building of your desire and longing, as sexual energy is the physical representation of what many have called the kundalini, the Chi, and many other names. This is something to remember and many people will not tell you in books teaching magickal practice, THERE IS NO MAGICK WITHOUT AROUSAL. Remember that you are channeling these feelings as they are part of the energetic vibration of your being and that counterparts to this react to within your mind and spirit even as your body has its own reactions physically.

When you are practicing the ritual itself you are leading towards the climax of the ritual which is the "sending" of the intent for its resultant manifestation. When you are in the midst of the ritual where you are speaking forth the "incantation" that you have created for the purpose of embodying your intent, switch your emotional state and your visualizations which accompany it from an intense longing to the satisfaction of having received/experienced the result of the intent fulfilled. This is very important because if you do not switch your emotions and visualization into the past tense at this point in your magickal working no matter what kind of ritual you are doing, it will always put the result of your magick out of your reach! The intense longing and desire that you have led up to all the way to this point in your actual magickal working has been much the same as the "foreplay" of a sexual act physically. This has the purpose of building the power and movement of your emotional state in the anchoring of your visualization so that you have the ability to effectively switch to this past tense mode where you are experiencing this within your mind (as well as your body and spirit) as having ALREADY HAPPENED. Just as physical sex is not very good for either partner under normal circumstances if no foreplay is involved, magick does not necessarily have the resultant power and effectiveness you would desire if you do not follow the steps to build yourself to the state of communication which the universe understands.

In this state that you switch to within this part of your ritual work, it is much like the orgasm in a sexual act. There is a release that takes place within the orgasm that is unlike any other. The tension of desire, the excitement and emotional buildup in many cases, all gets fired off (whether you are male or female) in the ecstasy of the final climax. Magick works the same way when you are "sending" your intent! Allow yourself to feel the experience of your intent realized as fully as possible with the same intensity as an orgasmic experience. If you are comfortable with it, you can also bring yourself to an actual physical orgasm while you are in this process as well. It is not necessary if you are able to allow yourself to experience "release" emotionally and in your visualizations but remember that the body must also be allowed to experience. This body experience does not have to be an actual orgasm, but it certainly can be if that is how you wish to augment and solidify your work.

Now to recap, I will illustrate this in a different way. Think of a battery that has the positive pole on one side and the negative pole in the other. It is necessary for there to be a flow of current for the battery to be used by any application. Think of the buildup that even starts before the ritual itself (the intense desire and longing for the fulfillment of your intent) as being the "negative pole" of your magickal battery. When you reach the climax of the ritual where you are speaking forth your will/intent and switch to the "past tense experience" of spirit mind and body of the working fulfilled as the positive pole of the battery. Once you have closed the circuit the magick than can flow.

Whether you are evoking a spirit, invoking a spirit, creating a talisman/amulet or even just doing a work with a free hand sigil that you have drawn yourself the entire process of sending the magickal force to bring about the manifestation of your will is the SAME! The context of your ritual may be different and the way that you perform it may vary from one experience to the next BUT the way that you charge your intent and send it forth has the same principle behind it because that is how you transmit your will through the "fluid" of the astral plane were all magick is done.

In the following chapters I am going to be going through a few different rituals that you can adapt and perform yourself. This book is not meant to be a grimoire, rather a manual of self-help for your ability to take any book that speaks of magickal rituals and effectively use it. I am going to be writing another book that is a grimoire filled with rituals from my own experience that you will be able to use and adapt as you wish and will be a great companion book to this work. My focus right now is to get you the reader into a place where you could succeed and have results in magical practice ranging from connecting to your own authentic self, to changing the very fabric of the reality of your life! Many of the things I have been talking about in this book are not talked about in a very clear usable manner and I hope that this book helps correct that problem.

Make sure that you have gone through the practices in the first parts of this book and have a clear confidence in yourself before using the rituals to follow.

NOTES

NOTES

Chapter 10: Evocation and Invocation

Many people in magical practice use "magic circles" to protect themselves when performing serious magical works. I do not follow this practice in every instance. Why? They are not nearly as effective in "protecting" you as they purport to be! Rather than using what many magicians almost religiously put forward, I leave that completely up to you.

You can use traditional ceremonial magic and perform the LBRP, or the "satanic circle" or any other modality that resonates with your practice. You can also take the "Centering/Banishing Ritual" that has been provided here in this book instead of any of those rituals.

The key in successfully working with spirits is RESPECT!! Do not try to arrogantly command them, rather choose to work WITH them in a partnership. If you work in this fashion unless you are dealing with a spirit that you really were not ready to work with (your intuition does tell you these things if you are listening) you will not have problems.

The spirits that are listed in this book, although powerful and definitely dangerous in their own way, are not a threat to you and in fact have no designs whatsoever to cause you issues AS LONG as you remember that word in capital letters within the previous paragraph, RESPECT.

Magical Incantations for Evocation

There are many ways to call forth spirits, but this is a way that I have found to be effective working with spirits of this kind. Please note as well that the sigils to follow are in color and are in my experience much easier to work with in this format. The colors are aligned to the elemental associations that I discovered the spirits are related to and will be just one more aid for the purpose of your focus.

Step one

- *in a place where you will not be disturbed set the sigil on whatever you are using for your altar*
- *spend about ten minutes gazing at the sigil while you focus on your breathing and the intent of your ritual*
- *when you intuitively feel the time has come to begin your call recite something like this:*

"By the power of my true self which is beyond understanding I do call upon the spirit (name of spirit) to manifest yourself to me in whatever way makes you tangible to my senses.

Come oh (name of spirit) by the power of IAO (EEEE-AAAAH-OOOOH), IHVI (Yod-Hey-Vahv-Heh), IVHI (Hey-Vahv-Hey-Yod), Abaddon (Ah-Bah-Don), and Ha'Shatan (Hah-Shah-Tan) Diabolous (Dee-Ah-Boh-Lohs)!

By darkness from which light doth spring forth in wisdom ineffable, come and manifest yourself to me now, and hear me in my requests.

IAO, IHVH, HVHI, Abaddon, Diabolous!!

Now, after you have done this begin to *chant the name of the spirit* as a mantra under your breath well your focus is completely absorbed in the sigil along with your intent which must be fraught with the emotion of your desire.

Please refer to this for each spirit as the formula is the same. There are other ways to invoke or evoke spirits, but this is what was communicated to me by the spirits listed within this book as their preferred way of being called forth.

You can also use other types of symbolism as you see fit depending upon what path of the arcane you are working with primarily. I will include some of the more common aspects of information here for you.

If you wish to use alchemical and elemental symbols along with the sigils that is perfectly fine. Below are some of the symbols that are used for the elements in Western ritual magic, along with alchemical symbols which of course are dealing with personal transformation.

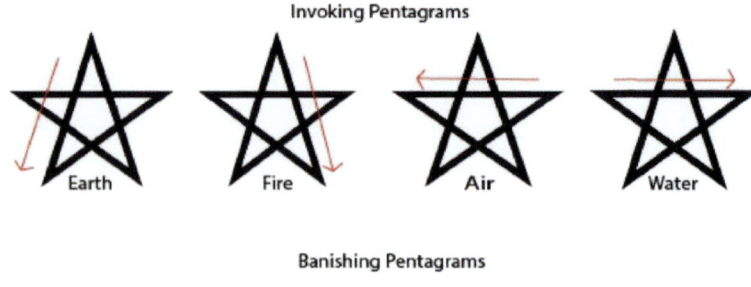

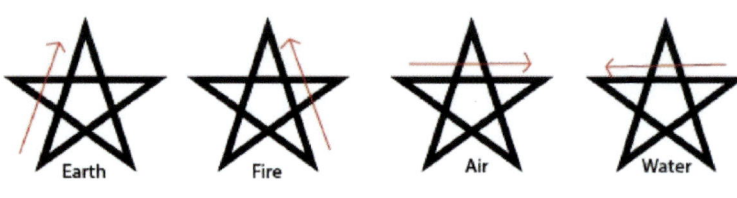

Invoking and Banishing Pentagrams

moon Luna	saltpetre	vinegar	ferrum
sun Sol	fire	mortar	iron vitriol
earth Terra	water	salt	lead
mercury Mercurius	air	antimony	white lead
venus Venus	earth	alcali	olive oil
mars Mars	copper	alumen	ammonia
jupiter Jupiter	lead	arsenic	salt
saturn Saturnus	brass	lapis lazuli	sulphuric acid
uranus Uranus	arsenic	copper saffron	sulphur
neptune Neptunus	phosphorus	copper acetate	potash
			transmutation

*** If you wish to do an **invocation** rather than an evocation the formula is the same apart from the way the manifestation is to take place. Please note the change in the underlined text of the incantation.*

"By the power of my true self which is beyond understanding I do call upon the spirit **(name of spirit)** to manifest yourself <u>**WITHIN**</u> me in whatever way makes you tangible to my senses in safety and clarity."

Please note These spirits are NOT from the "dimensions" of tomes such as the Goetia. They are from a "place" for lack of a better word that is BEYOND dualism (which is why many will appear as androgynous) though they may appear as "male" or "female" as it suits them. In working with them, the spirits communicated that the details of their expression in consciousness is "diminished" for the purpose of being "understandable" at least in part to the limited minds of human awareness. My experience with them in working with more "classical" spirits, is that the spirits in general which inhabit our planes of consciousness cower in their presence! A legitimate (from my experience with the individual) magician once told me in their ritual work with me, that these spirits (among many others I work with and will share in future works that are actually dedicated grimoires) were like "gods" even to gods/esses themselves.

There IS also a physical toll that I have experienced working with this class of spirit. I have found in my own work with these spirits (and others on this strata) that there are effects on the nervous system, other times the body just "gives out" for a period of time resulting in passing out in ritual. You may find different experiences but being fore-warned is being fore-armed.

This is not because the spirits are hostile to anyone without a cause, rather that the energy of their presence is more than the body can deal with at times. Upon request during the ritual to work with them, you can ask for them to further "shield" their aura so that you can work with them more effectively.

Why do I put a few of THESE type of spirits into a work like this? Primarily because they will HELP the reader if worked with in deep respect, to PURGE and re-build the psyche in a way that avoids many pitfalls that can sideline any magician.

Please take these notes seriously, and you will find that success will be in your grasp within ways you never thought possible.

The Spirit Belatry

Name: Belatry

Title: unknown

Elemental Association: Water

This King has power over the subconscious mind in general and this includes the realm of "dreams" Belatry can help in processing information vital to your awareness and often appears as an androgynous being. Belatry's level of consciousness can be extremely disconcerting to the ill prepared. There is no room for self-deception in the presence of Belatry as that type of dishonesty will be shredded without mercy so bear that in mind when you call upon the spirit.

Belatry can help with the understanding of your own subconscious imagery, and as well can help increase your intuitive ability when dealing with others. The gaze of Belatry is extremely sharp and piercing! Those abilities he is willing to give to you for certain periods of time if you are in alignment with self-transformation. Obviously, you can see how useful he is (or it as he appears often as stated earlier as an androgynous being) where it comes to dealing with the deprogramming process in the first part of this book.

Depending on the circumstances you may find yourself calling upon Belatry, he can also send dreams to other people on your behalf. The intuitive and deep state of consciousness that Belatry resides on is a powerful force leading towards the development and honing of your own abilities to "dream walk" and send messages subconsciously to other people in the manipulation of circumstances to your own benefit. He is a great companion to have with you if you are involved in any type of career that deals with people.

He can also send horrific nightmares to your enemies and cause them to believe falsehoods about themselves which he then shreds with all the emotional turmoil that that brings about if folks have identified with his deceptions as truth. This almost invariably happens unless you are dealing with someone who is well-versed in the occult. If you find yourself in the position of having to use Belatry's power for defence or revenge, do not forget that emphasis of your own personal transformation or you may end up as well becoming embroiled in turmoil because of the above-mentioned reasons.

The Spirit Belatry

The Spirit Molichni

Name: Morlichni ("ch" pronounced as in "Loch")

Title: Unknown

Elemental Association: Fire

The power of Morlichni is "aggressive defence"! Call this spirit with wisdom as his work can be DEADLY!

He wields the power of the element of fire in its aspect of the type of destruction which happens BEFORE creation can occur. The power of Morlichni if used on a person or a group can result in the destruction of the said person or group in extremely painful ways. I include this spirit here because I know there are different circumstances that people find themselves in where aggressive defence is something that would be a great help. Use the wisdom of your inner Daemon if you find you must use Morlichni for this purpose.

In the aspect of personal transformation Morlichni can show you directly what needs to be expunged from your psyche in order to grow in connection to your Daemon. A word of warning, that Morlichni can cause havoc in your life if you refuse to acknowledge the things, he reveals due to self-deception. Be honest with yourself to a fault if you are working with Morlichni with growth in mind.

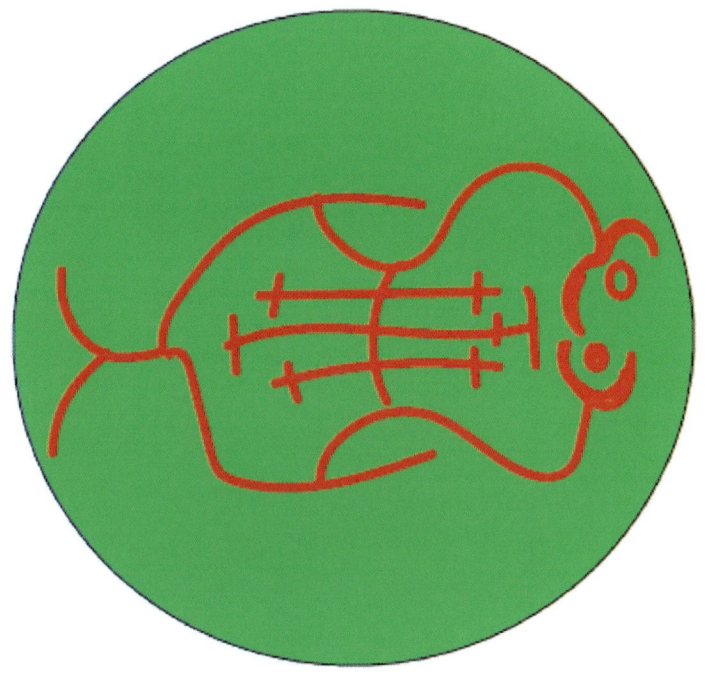

The Spirit Morlichni

The Spirit Tarak

Name: Tarak

Title: Unknown

Elemental Association: Air

Tarak is a spirit that often reveals itself in a female form and is one of those spirits that will often act as a "mentor" to those wishing deeper experience in the arcane. Self-honesty is again of paramount importance as you can deceive yourself easily with her if you are even subconsciously hiding the truth from yourself. It is for this reason that many of the spirits need to be worked with in conjunction with one another and not necessarily "one at a time". This does NOT mean evoking more than one spirit in a magical rite but evoking the spirits throughout the course of a month working with all of them as they complement one another.

Call on Tarak to learn greater effectiveness and magick through DEEP AWARENESS of how magick works along with your quest and remembering who and what you really are in connection to the infinite itself. This is more than just intuitive knowledge, but practical within the scope of your understanding because the element of air does relate itself very much to thought processes within both the conscious and subconscious mind. It is not as deep as elemental water, but it is a complement to the intuitive knowledge that you receive from the depths of the abyss.

The Spirit Tarak

The Spirit Perasin

Name: Perasin

Title: Unknown

Elemental Association: Water

Perasin is a gentle, but unforgiving spirit the deals with the emotional currents of the astral plane. The power of emotion, and intuition are not the "absolute", but they are definitely the "currency" of the astral plane in all its levels. As with many spirits, Perasin feeds on this and can also teach the practitioner how to feed on these energies as well. A side effect of this practice is the extension of control over one's OWN emotional state-and being able to use emotion more effectively in magical ritual and for actions of directed will.

If insulted, Perasin can and will feed off the magician and is very difficult to banish! Just a word to the wise, when dealing with spirits in any situation courtesy and respect goes a long way. Just forget about all those books that tell you how you must "command" the spirits as that is more of an intrusion of religious theology into the arcane.

The secret of "vampirism" in its purest state are also on the threshold of what Perasin teaches as well. Work with Perasin wisely.

The Spirit Perasin

The Spirit Zetanach

Name: Zetanach ("CH" pronounced like a hard "K")

Title: Prince

Elemental Association: Air

Zetanach is an interesting spirit to work with as he is from another realm of evolution entirely. He is very useful in bringing awareness of the "big picture" and how the "little picture" of our limited perceptions can be deceiving to us. He can help exponentially in understanding arcane secrets that bear not only on personal transformation, but on the understanding of how things work in the natural order of what we know as the universe.

Of all the spirit is listed here Zetanach is one of the best natured and easy to work with within the process outlined in the first part of this book. He gives truthful answers when questioned although many times he does speak in riddles if we are allowing ourselves to identify too much with the temporal limited world rather than our Daemon-almost as though he is "chiding" the magician rather than being deliberately deceptive. The key to working with Zetanach is the deliberate choice of will to identify with the "big picture" and that which lies beyond it (even if we are not sure how depending on the stage of our personal development) as that seems to be enough for Zetanach to clarify himself and to work with the magician.

The Spirit Zetanach

NOTES

NOTES

NOTES

NOTES

Epilogue

Please note that this book is not officially a "grimoire" and the spirits that are listed in the second section of the book are meant to give you some practical experience in working with spirits that will be of help to you in the process outlined in the first section of the book. This is also NOT an "academic" book, rather a WORKING book for your own experience.

There are many people that honestly believe that they have not been subjected to "mental programming" yet there is not a single one of us that has not been programmed since the time we were born, and exposed to that programming even today as adults. The question that we need to ask ourselves is not "have we been mentally programmed?" But "how do we take control of our minds back so that we are not swept away with manipulative narratives meant to subjugate us?". This is all part of self-honesty and understanding the way things **are**, rather than what we have been told that they are – or what we have wished that they would be. It is only through getting to that stage were true change can occur!

Do not rush through the process is outlined in this book. Allow yourself to have the opportunity to work through things in a way that is effective to your unique challenges in life. Through doing this you will find yourself moving from a sense of being "controlled" by apparent outward circumstance, to becoming an effective architect of your own experience in life under the direction of your own will.

The way that I wrote this book was as a conversation based upon the experience and magick that I have had in at this point in my life is approximately thirty-five years. Most of what I have done has not been based upon the writings of any other magician with the exception of course of things that I did very early on. My hope for you is that as you move forward into effective magical practice and that you also move away from parroting other magician's views so as to begin to experiencing the confidence that comes from your own practice. This does not take away from the work of other magicians which are of course a great help to anyone practicing in the arcane. What I am saying is that if ALL YOU DO is "parrot" other magicians work, the time will come when you will find yourself **not** actually in connection with the authenticity of your own Daemon. What I will have at the end of this book is an appendix rather than a bibliography, where you will see links to work I have done online on our public YouTube channel; work that I have available on our website; a place where you can effectively learn the transcendent principles of magick on an ongoing community basis.

Thank you so much for going through and reading this book! Give yourself the chance and go through the practices that are within its pages.

In Sincerity,

Daniel Updike

Important Resources

Website:

https://tdpvideocast.com

Tools and Downloads:

https://tdpvideocast.com/tools-and-downloads

Teaching Community:

https://www.patreon.com/TDPVideocasts

YouTube Channel:

https://www.youtube.com/channel/UChxJ1A83mIz4oo7ZHFyDxow

When we with brutal self-honesty turn our gaze inward, we in a PROCESS begin to embody "what is" warts and all. This enables and empowers us to begin the process of ACTUAL transformation which makes a difference not from the outside in, but the INSIDE out!

**The artwork displayed from "Kelly-Kelly" was commissioned by me for this book. I gave her an idea of what I was trying to communicate, and through her own occult practice and intuition she produced the art both for the cover and in the noted illustrations. **

You can find her work online at this link:

https://www.facebook.com/kellykellyart/

If you wish to contact Kelly for artwork that you would like created, you can communicate with her via the page linked above or through the email address: kelly.kelly.arts@gmail.com

About the Author

Daniel Updike was born on December 11, 1968 into the home of a devout Pentecostal preacher. He was raised within the evangelical environment and was trained theologically as a minister himself.

From the early age of four years old, Daniel experienced paranormal phenomenon including the artistic inspiration to "draw" what in later investigation turned out to be eighteen of the twenty-nine classical Anglo-Saxon Futhorc runes. This tension between the dogmatic assertions of evangelical theology, and the continual anomalous experiences that seem to contradict these assertions, went on until Daniel was in his mid-teens. At that time Daniel began to research paranormal phenomenon, the runes of the Germanic tribes, and the practice of ritual magic. This was kept secret from those within his family for obvious reasons.

In his early 20s Daniel began to work exclusively with occult practice centered on Hermeticism; Ceremonial Magic; the practices of Rune Magic and Seidhr. This led him down many "rabbit holes" and through both successes and failures brought him to the place where an understanding (in a way that is possible within the universe of limitation) of what we really are as sentiment beings within this multiverse – and beyond!

After a devastating experience while at work in Northern Alberta, in which he had his heart deliberately stopped at the hospital as a (last ditch effort to correct a problem he had experienced since birth) there was a desire on Daniel's part to impart some of the things that he had been able to learn so that others may be able to benefit from and perhaps even create their own system of personal growth.

Daniel is always said that he was better at doing video productions and audio broadcasts than writing, but regardless of which this book has been written for your benefit and hopefully it is something that you will be able to use successfully in your growth! To hear more and to experience more, please refer to the YouTube channel and website that are in the resources section at the end of this book.

Daniel and his wife practice magic together and are currently residing in Alberta Canada.

**To contact the author, email The TDP Videocast at:

host@tdpvideocasts.com

Printed in Poland
by Amazon Fulfillment
Poland Sp. z o.o., Wrocław

50058663R00091